I Know I Am Loved

by Dolores Mize
photography by Angela Talentino

Life Cycle Books
Niagara Falls, NY • Toronto, ON

Published by:

Life Cycle Books
PO Box 1008
Niagara Falls, NY 14304-1008

Phone: (800) 214-5849
Fax: (888) 690-8532

e-mail: orders@lifecyclebooks.com
www.lifecyclebooks.com

Canadian office:
Life Cycle Books Ltd.
1149 Bellamy Rd., Unit 20
Toronto, ON M1H 1H7

Printed in Canada   ISBN # 978-0-919225-35-0

For my friend, Jesus.

To: Anthony,

    my Trail Blazer

Joseph,

    my Tender Heart

Margaret,

    my Morning Glory

Jonathan,

    my Joyful Lamb

and my dear husband, Brian

With Love.

D.M.

For my clients.

Thank you for allowing me to

share in your joys.

And for my girls: Denise, Jen,

Missy, Kristie and Julie.

I am blessed to have you all

in my life. Thank you for

sharing my vision.

Much Love,

A.T.

In the *silence* of darkness,

I can feel a steady *pushing*.

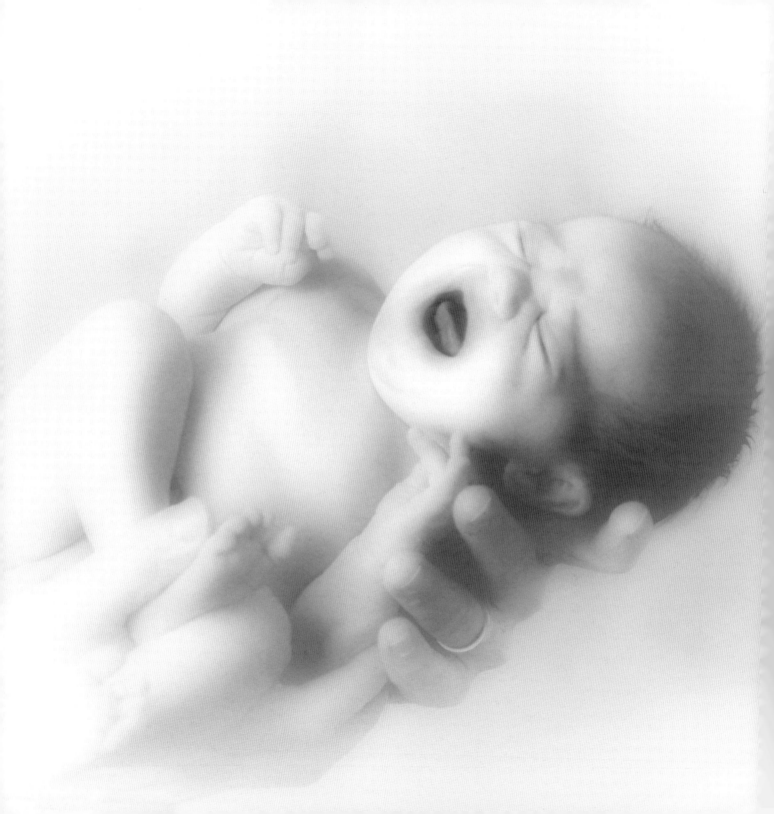

Suddenly, I sense a new surrounding.

It's *bright*

and noisy and cold.

I am *born!*

I open my mouth
and with one
bold gasp,

I fill my lungs and
cry
to announce
my presence.

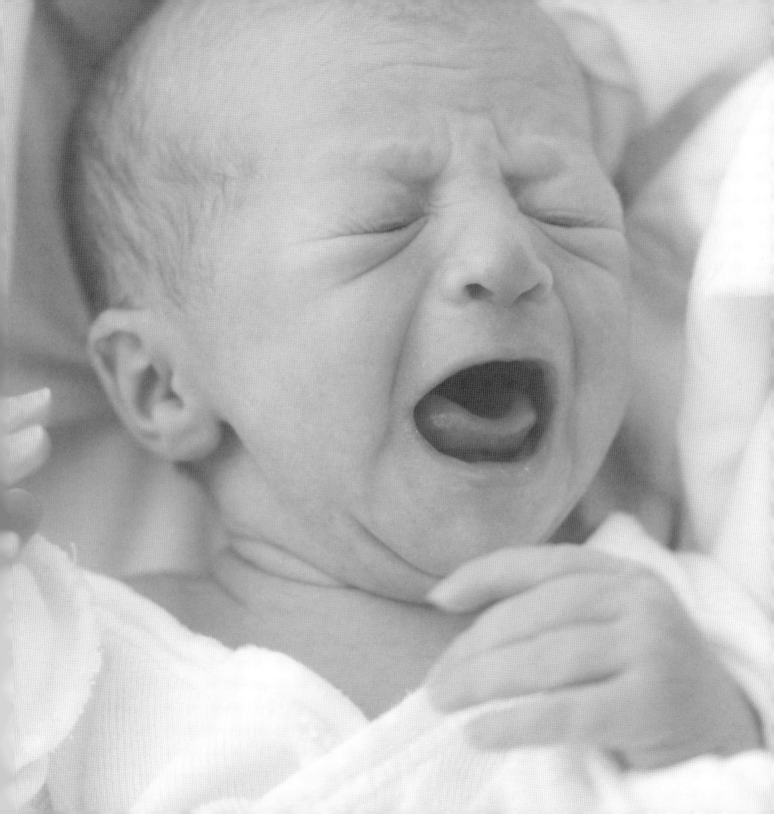

Kind hands *gently* cleanse me, then wrap me *snuggly* in the warmth of soft blankets.

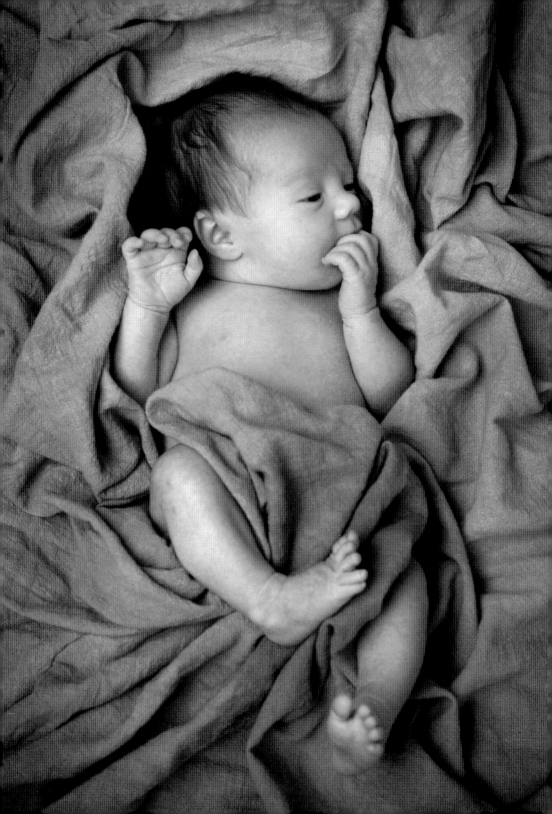

I hear the *happy* cries of joy from my **mother.**

She sounds so filled with *love* and **wonder.**

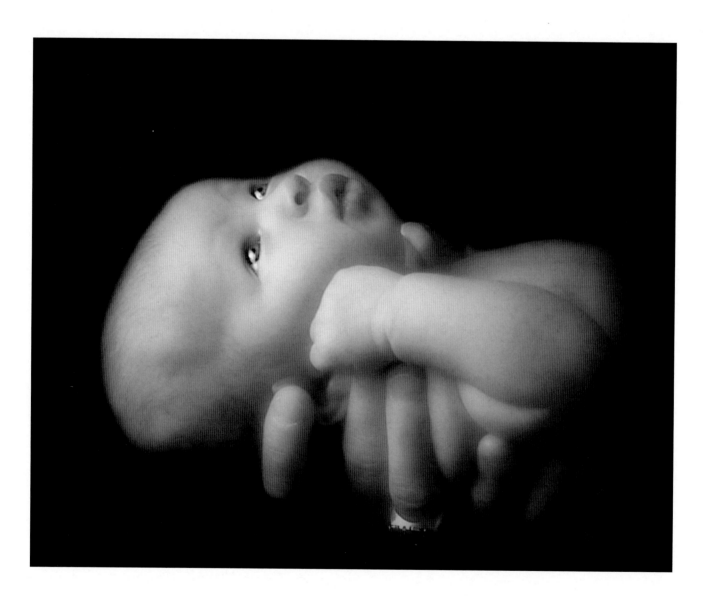

I hear the *proud* voice of my father.

I turn my head towards the voice and see a *glimpse* of Daddy's *beaming* face.

I've *dreamed*
of you, Daddy.

I know
you!

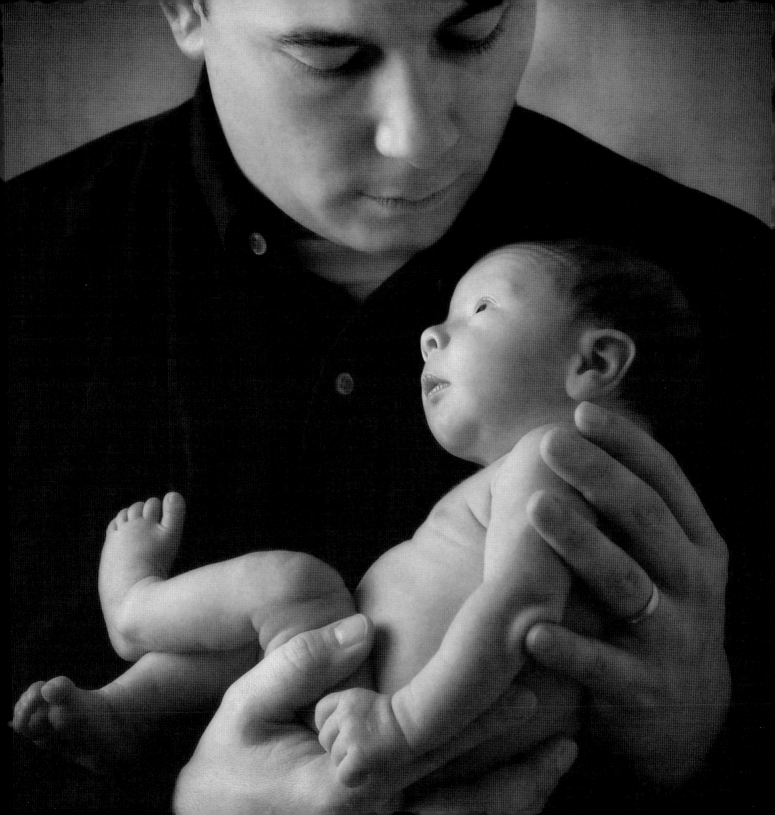

In a moment I'm placed in

tender arms,

I cuddle in

close

and hear a familiar

heartbeat.

Mommy

holds me.

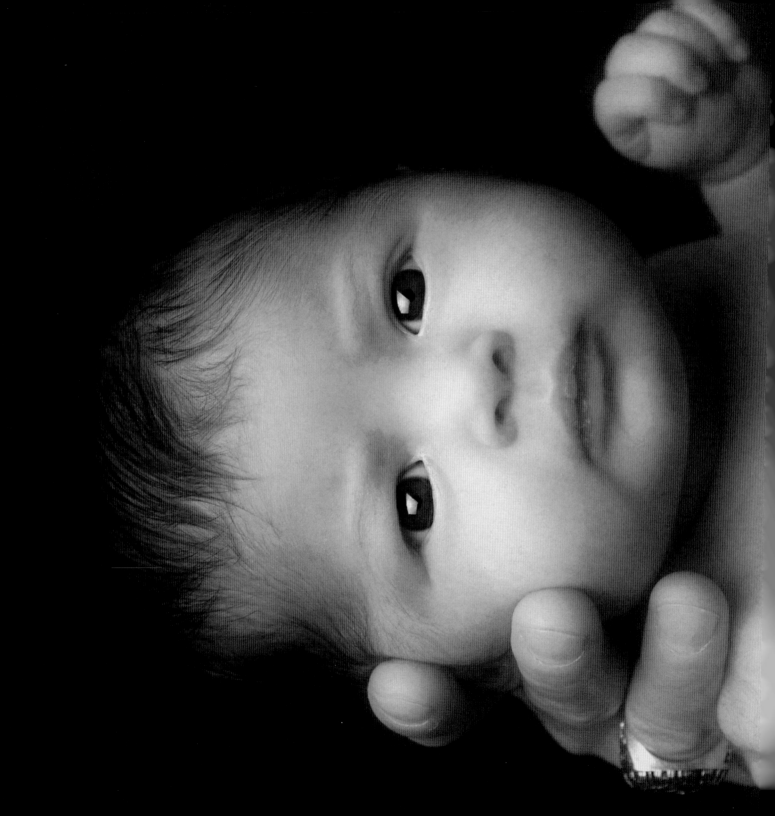

I've longed to see you

Mommy.

I Love You!

Gentle
murmurs fill my ears
and my face is covered with
Mommy's
soft kisses.

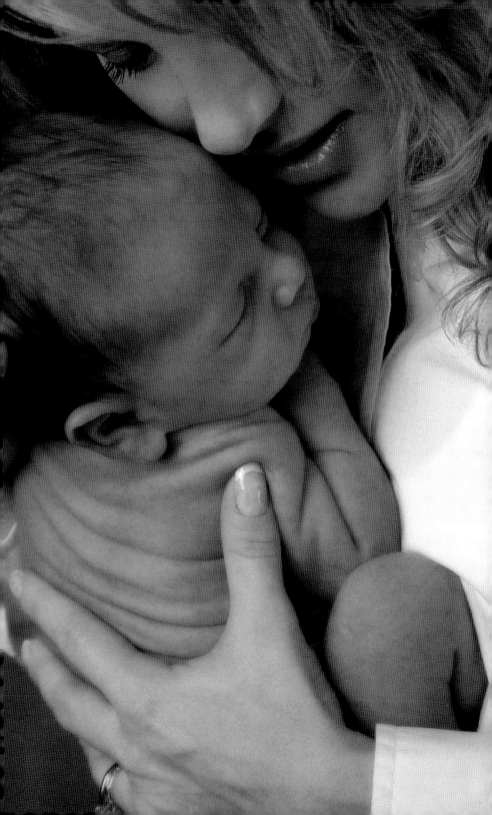

With *quivering* fingers,

Daddy *caresses*

my cheek and strokes my

baby fine hair.

All around me the *angels* sing for *joy,* while *God* my Father *smiles.*

I've waited all my *life* for this **wonderful** moment.

I couldn't possibly be *happier!*

For above all things,

I *know* I am

loved.

I have loved you
with an

everlasting
love;

I have drawn
you with *loving*
kindness.
Jeremiah 31:3

Every good and *perfect* gift is from above, coming down from the *Father* of the heavenly lights.

James 1:17

My special love story...

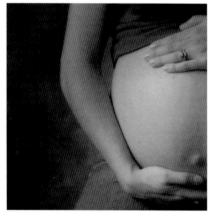 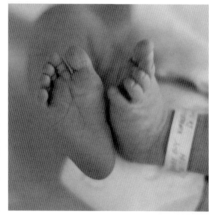 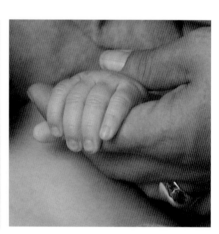

My Mommy and Daddy
found out they were
expecting a baby!

Me!

How Mommy and Daddy
shared the happy news...

They're
expecting me!

Thoughts and memories about *visits* to the doctor...

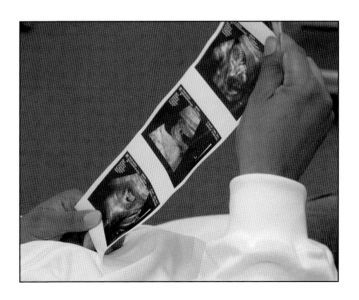

Exciting events
leading up to my
birth...

My big day has finally arrived!

Here I come!

date of birth: _____

weight: _____

length: _____

birth place: _____

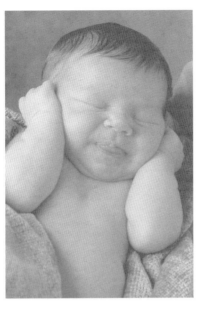 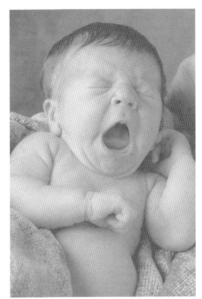

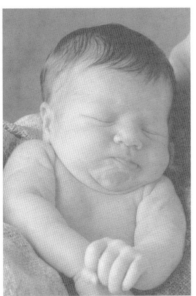 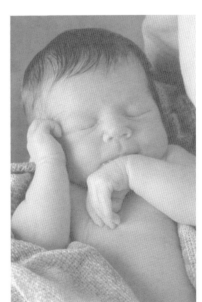

Loving thoughts from Mommy

Loving thoughts from

Daddy...

My family welcomes me home.